G000255131

Collins

AQA GCSE 9-1
Food Preparation and Nutrition

Workbook

Fiona Balding, Barbara Monks,
Barbara Rathmill and
Suzanne Gray with Louise T. Davies

Preparing for the GCSE Exam

Revision That Really Works

Experts have found that there are two techniques that help you to retain and recall information and consistently produce better results in exams compared to other revision techniques.

It really isn't rocket science either – you simply need to:

- **test yourself** on each topic as many times as possible
- **leave a gap** between the test sessions.

Three Essential Revision Tips

1. **Use Your Time Wisely**
   - Allow yourself plenty of time.
   - Try to start revising at least six months before your exams – it's more effective and less stressful.
   - Don't waste time re-reading the same information over and over again – it's not effective!

2. **Make a Plan**
   - Identify all the topics you need to revise.
   - Plan at least five sessions for each topic.
   - One hour should be ample time to test yourself on the key ideas for a topic.
   - Spread out the practice sessions for each topic – the optimum time to leave between each session is about one month but, if this isn't possible, just make the gaps as big as realistically possible.

3. **Test Yourself**
   - Methods for testing yourself include: quizzes, practice questions, flashcards, past papers, explaining a topic to someone else, etc.
   - Don't worry if you get an answer wrong – provided you check what the correct answer is, you are more likely to get the same or similar questions right in future!

Visit **collins.co.uk/collinsGCSErevision** for more information about the benefits of these techniques, and for further guidance on how to plan ahead and make them work for you.

Command Words Used in Exam Questions

This table shows the meanings of some of the most commonly used command words in GCSE exam questions.

Command word	Meaning
State.../Give...	Write the facts clearly and briefly, giving your answer from recall.
Name...	Write the correct name or term.
Which...	Choose the correct option from the information given.
Describe...	Give clear characteristics in sufficient detail.
Explain...	Write a detailed answer using appropriate terminology to give reasons.
Discuss...	Write about the different points of view or the strengths and weaknesses. Give the key points about the topic.
Compare...	Write about the similarities and differences in the information you are given.
Suggest...	Present ideas that are reasonable and sensible.
Complete...	Add to a task to finalise or finish it off.
Interpret...	Understand and make sense of the information provided to answer the question.
Review...	Interpret and evaluate the information given.

Contents

1 Which type of knife is shown in the picture? Tick the correct answer.

a) Paring knife ☐

b) Filleting knife ☐

c) Cook's knife ☐

d) Palette knife ☐

[1]

2 When preparing meat, what colour cutting board should be used? Tick the correct answer.

a) Blue ☐

b) Green ☐

c) Brown ☐

d) Red ☐

[1]

3 Explain three important safety rules to observe when using knives for preparing different foods.

Safety Rule 1: ....

Reason: ....

Safety Rule 2: ....

Reason: ....

Safety Rule 3: ....

Reason: ....

[6]

4 Good knife skills are the foundation of many cooking techniques to produce high quality dishes. Name and describe the two main methods of cutting that are the basis of a cook's knife-handling skills.

	Knife Hold: ....
	Explanation: ....
	Knife Hold: ....
	Explanation: ....

[4]

Total Marks .... / 12

1 Which of the following fish would you expect to find preserved in a can? Tick the correct answer.

a) Cod ☐   b) Plaice ☐

c) Salmon ☐   d) Halibut ☐   [1]

2 Which choice would **not** be suitable when enrobing a fish fillet before cooking? Tick the correct answer.

a) Breadcrumbs ☐   b) Polenta ☐

c) Batter ☐   d) Roux sauce ☐   [1]

3 Complete the following statements using the words below.

collagen	60 °C	coagulate	muscle	gelatine	connective tissue

Fish cooks quickly because the .... is short and the

.... is thin.

The connective tissue is made up of .... and will change into

.... and .... at ....   [6]

4 Answer the questions about the fish shown.

a) What is the classification of the fish? .... [1]

b) Give one example of this type of fish. .... [1]

c) What type of knife should be used to prepare this fish? .... [1]

d) What colour chopping board should be used to prepare this fish? .... [1]

e) Explain how you would fillet this fish.

....

....

....

....   [3]

Total Marks .... / 15

1 Which of these nutrients is **not** found in meat? Tick the correct answer.

a) Fat ☐ b) Calcium ☐

c) Vitamin B6 ☐ d) Vitamin E ☐ [1]

2 Which meat is classed as game? Tick the correct answer.

a) Duck ☐ b) Beef ☐

c) Pheasant ☐ d) Chicken ☐ [1]

3 Some meats cuts are more tender than others. Name one cut of meat that is tough and discuss two different methods that could be used for cooking to ensure it is tender.

_____

_____

_____

_____ [3]

4 What colour board should be used to prepare raw meat? _____ [1]

5 Name two methods of tenderising meat.

_____

_____ [2]

6 Complete the following sentences about what happens when meat is cooked. Use the words below.

| Maillard | gelatine | coagulate | browning | sugars |

The _____ of meat is caused by a reaction with natural _____ and

proteins to produce a dark colour. This occurrence is called the _____ reaction or

non-enzymic browning.

As the meat cooks, the proteins _____ and produce a firm texture. Collagen is

broken down into _____. [5]

Total Marks _____ / 13

1 Which glaze would be most suitable for plain bread rolls? Tick the correct answer.

a) Egg wash ☐   b) Sugar and water ☐

c) Arrowroot glaze ☐   d) Salt water ☐   [1]

2 The following sentences describe the technique of folding in flour.

Choose the correct words from the boxes to complete the sentences.

| combine | figure-of-eight | texture | mix | cake | retains |

Folding and stirring are methods used to .... and ....

ingredients. Folding is different to stirring because it is a careful .... movement

used for adding flour when .... making. Folding .... air in a

cake mixture, which helps the cooked cake to have a light, airy ....   [6]

3 Biscuits and some types of bread need skilled handling and special techniques to achieve their distinctive shapes.

a) Which piece of equipment would ensure consistent even thickness for biscuits?

....   [1]

b) The picture shows Palmier biscuits. Name the two techniques used to achieve their shape.

....   [2]

c) The picture shows Viennese whirl biscuits. What method is used to achieve their shape?

....   [2]

d) The picture shows some wholegrain bread rolls.
What methods would be used to achieve their shape?

....   [3]

Total Marks .... / 15

1 a) How can pasta dough be rolled consistently and evenly?

.... [1]

b) After pasta is rolled, cut and left to air dry, what changes occur?

.... [2]

2 Which one of the following would be the best choice of flour for making pasta dough? Tick the correct answer.

a) Self-raising wheat flour ☐   **b)** '00' Durum wheat flour ☐

c) Cornflour ☐   **d)** Gram flour ☐

e) Rice flour ☐   [1]

3 Name two ingredients that could be successfully used to add colour to pasta dough.

Ingredient: ....   Colour achieved: ....

Ingredient: ....   Colour achieved: ....   [4]

4 Flour-based mixtures are popular when learning to cook. Circle which of the following are flour-based recipes.   [3]

Omelette   Pastry   Porridge   Bread   Pasta   Risotto   Ratatouille

5 Choux pastry contains fat. Explain how the fat is prepared to be added to the flour.

....

.... [2]

6 Shortcrust pastry is made with a ratio of half fat to flour. True or False?

.... [1]

Total Marks .... / 14

Protein and Fat

1. Proteins are formed from units called a... a... . [2]

2. **a)** Give three good sources of plant protein.

   ....

   .... [3]

   b) Circle two of the following dishes that would be a good protein source for a lacto vegetarian.

   Fish Pie   **Cauliflower Cheese**   **Chicken and Chickpea Curry**

   Mushroom and Lentil Bake
   [2]

3. What is Protein Complementation? Give an example.

   ....

   ....

   .... [2]

4. Fats are made of f................................. a................................. and g................................. . [2]

5. Saturated fats can increase what level in the blood? Tick the correct answer.
   a) Iron $\square$
   b) Blood sugar $\square$
   c) Cholesterol $\square$
   d) Amino acids $\square$
   [1]

6. Give three examples of foods which are high in unsaturated fat.

   ....

   ....

   .... [3]

Total Marks .... / 15

1 The main function of carbohydrate in the body is to provide ....   [1]

2 Carbohydrates are produced mainly by plants during what process? Circle the correct answer.

Osmosis   Dextrinisation   Photosynthesis   Caramelisation   [1]

3 A lack of fibre in the diet can cause the medical condition constipation. Explain what this condition is.

....

....

....   [2]

4 How much dietary fibre is recommended for an adult every day? Tick the correct answer.

a) A least 6 g   ☐   b) At least 10 g   ☐

c) At least 18 g   ☐   d) At least 30 g   ☐   [1]

5 Carbohydrates can be classified according to their structure.

Those structures are:

M...

D...

P...   [3]

6 Explain why starches provide slow-release energy in the body.

....

....

....   [2]

7 Discuss the health implications of consuming too much carbohydrate.

....

....

....

....   [3]

Total Marks .... / 13

Food Nutrition and Health

Vitamins

1 Name three dietary sources of Vitamin C.

....

....

.... [3]

2 Which vitamin can be made in the body by the action of sunlight on the skin?

Tick the correct answer.

a) Vitamin B1 ☐

b) Vitamin D ☐

c) Vitamin A ☐

d) Vitamin E ☐ [1]

3 Spina bifida has been linked to a lack of which vitamin, both pre and during pregnancy?

.... [1]

4 Water soluble Vitamins B and C can be lost easily during food preparation and cooking. Suggest three ways to maximise vitamin retention.

....

....

....

.... [3]

5 The table below lists five vitamins. Give one function of each.

Vitamin	Function
Vitamin A	
Vitamin K	
Vitamin C	
Vitamin D	
Vitamin B1	

[5]

Total Marks .... / 13

1 Vitamin C assists with the absorption of which mineral in the body? Underline the correct answer.

Calcium   Iodine   Sodium   Iron   [1]

2 Fill in the missing words to complete the sentence.

Iron supports the production of h.. in red blood cells, which transport

o.. around the body.   [2]

3 **a)** Lack of water, particularly during hot weather, can cause what condition?

.... [1]

b) Give three functions of water in the body.

....

....

.... [3]

4 Two deficiency diseases associated with a lack of calcium in the diet are:

R.. in children.

O.. in older people.   [2]

5 Give three good sources of iron in the diet.

....

....

.... [3]

Total Marks .... / 12

Making Informed Choices

1 Referring to the Eatwell Guide, which two sections are the largest?

....

.... [2]

2 Fill in the missing words to complete the sentence.

For breast-fed babies, the first milk that a mother produces is called c...

and it is full of a... . [2]

3 Why is iron-deficiency anaemia common in teenage girls?

....

....

.... [2]

4 Older people require a good supply of calcium in the diet to help prevent which condition?
Underline the correct answer.

Anaemia **Scurvy** **Dementia** **Osteoporosis** [1]

5 Name two plant sources of protein that could be found in the pink section of the Eatwell Guide.

....

.... [2]

6 It is important that pregnant women have a healthy diet. Name three nutrients that they need to
increase their consumption of, and explain why they are important for the developing baby.

....

....

....

....

....

.... [6]

Total Marks _____ / 15

1 Fill in the missing word.

_____ is an abnormal accumulation of body fat. [1]

2 What is used as a measurement in adults to see if they are a healthy weight for their height?

_____ [1]

3 Explain why elderly people require a good supply of calcium and Vitamin D.

_____

_____

_____ [2]

4 The risk of bowel cancer can be reduced by increasing what in the diet? Circle the correct answer.

Sugar   **Fibre/NSP**   **Protein**   **Vitamin C** [1]

5 Explain the damage that can be caused to children's teeth as a result of a high sugar diet.

_____

_____

_____

_____ [2]

6 Give three symptoms of iron-deficient anaemia.

_____

_____

_____ [3]

7 Fill in the missing words to complete the sentences.

In Type 2 d_____, too little or no i_____ is produced in the

p_____ resulting in high levels of s_____ in the b_____. [5]

Total Marks _____ / 15

1 A chef has to decide between oven-roasting a range of vegetables or boiling the same vegetables. What characteristics would be different after cooking in each way?

Oven-roasted Vegetables	Boiled Vegetables

[4]

2 What is the correct heat transfer method for frying onions? Tick the correct answer.

a) Conduction ☐   b) Convection ☐

c) Radiation ☐   d) Induction ☐   [1]

3 Boiled potatoes can be mashed and layered over a meat mixture, such as in cottage pie. Which cooking method and heat transfer method would change the plain mashed potato topping to become golden brown and crisp?

.... [2]

4 A menu in a restaurant offers poached salmon and marinated chicken thighs.

a) Describe the main effect of poaching the salmon.   [2]

....

b) State the main reasons for marinating the chicken thighs.

.... [2]

5 Complete the following sentences using the words given below.

| sticking | convection | heat | conduction | thickening |

When making a sauce, heat is transferred from the hob through the base of the pan by

.... and through the sauce by .... Stirring prevents

.... on the base of the pan and distributes .... to aid

....   [5]

Total Marks .... / 16

1 When making a pear flan with fresh fruit, the topping starts to turn brown.

a) Explain why the pears turn brown.

....

.... [2]

b) Suggest what could stop the browning of the pears.

.... [1]

2 Bread and butter pudding is an affordable and nutritious pudding. Buttered bread is soaked in an egg custard mixture before cooking.

a) State two changes that would be seen when the pudding is cooked.

....

.... [2]

b) Explain how and why the egg and milk custard is changed by the cooking.

....

....

....

.... [4]

3 a) Name the enzyme present in fresh pineapple.

.... [1]

b) What purpose would fresh pineapple have if used in a marinade for prawns before cooking?

.... [1]

4 Which of the following would reduce oxidation occurring when cooking vegetables? Tick the correct answers.

a) Using bicarbonate of soda in the cooking water ☐

b) Using a lid on the pan when boiling vegetables ☐

c) Using quicker short methods of cooking such as microwave or stir-fry ☐ [2]

5 Which protein helps a dough to be stretchy and elastic? Circle the correct answer. [1]

Glucose   **Glycerine**   **Gluten**   **Glycerol**

Total Marks .... / 14

Carbohydrates

1 A recipe asks for onions to be sliced and fried gently until golden. What are the reasons for this?

....

....

.... [3]

2 a) When making soup from vegetables and a stock, name two different starches that could be used as thickeners.

.... [2]

b) Explain how starch can thicken a liquid.

....

....

.... [3]

3 When making toast, describe how sensory factors are changed because of grilling.

....

.... [2]

4 a) What are the reasons for a roux sauce being stirred throughout preparation?

....

....

.... [4]

b) Which two methods of sauce making bring about gelatinisation of starch? Tick the two correct answers.

i) Emulsification ☐

ii) Blending ☐

iii) Reduction ☐

iv) Roux ☐

[2]

Total Marks .... / 16

1 Here is a shortbread recipe. Explain the functions of the baking fat in this recipe.

> 150 g flour
>
> 100 g baking fat (yellow fat)
>
> 50 g caster sugar

....

....

....

.... [4]

2 When using baking fat, such as butter, temperature plays an important role.

a) Insert the following food preparation methods in the correct place in the table. [3]

Creaming   **Rubbing-in**   **Melting method**

Temperature of Fat	Food Preparation Method	Example of Dish
Chilled temperature		
Room temperature		
Warm pan temperature		

b) Complete the chart by giving an example of a dish made using each preparation method.

[3]

3 a) When making cakes, why is aeration so important? Give two reasons.

....

.... [2]

b) Name two cake preparation methods that aerate mixtures effectively.

....

.... [2]

4 What sort of foam is achieved when a creaming method is successfully prepared?

.... [1]

Total Marks .... / 15

1 **a)** A student is researching mechanical (physical) methods of raising agents by preparing a range of dishes.

Complete the list in the table below by naming a recipe and linking it to a method of trapping air. The first one has been done for you:

Recipe/Product Name	Mechanical (Physical) Method to Trap Air
Pastry	Rubbing-in technique

[4]

b) Name and give an example of one other classification of raising agents that is **not** biological.

....

[2]

2 Choose the most likely raising method from the list below, for successful use in the preparation of the products in the table.

Steam production   Beating   S.R. flour   Baking powder

Product	Raising Agent
Victoria sandwich	
Muffins	
English pancakes	
Choux buns	

[4]

3 Which raising agent is particularly likely to give a soapy taste to products?

....

[1]

4 What type of foam does egg white produce when whisked?

....

[1]

5 What is baking powder?

....

....

[4]

Total Marks .... / 16

1 Name two microorganisms that can cause food spoilage.

[2]

2 Give three factors that affect the rate of microbial growth.

[3]

3 Identify three signs that could show if food has spoiled.

[3]

4 Suggest three ways to store dry food, such as flour, in order to stop it from spoiling.

[3]

5 Suggest two ways in which oxidation (enzymic browning), as shown in the picture, can be prevented.

[2]

Total Marks _____ / 13

Microorganisms in Food Production

1 Complete the following sentences using the words below.

probiotic	harmful	digestion	single	rapidly

cheese	food poisoning

Bacteria are _____-celled organisms, which are able to reproduce

_____. Some are _____ and cause _____

or even death. Some are harmless and used in _____-making.

_____ bacteria help _____.   [7]

2 Discuss the positive uses of the following microorganisms on food production. Use examples in your answer.

a) Moulds

_____

_____

_____

_____

_____

_____   [4]

b) Bacteria

_____

_____

_____

_____

_____

_____   [4]

3 Starter cultures are used to make dried, fermented meat products. Give three examples of these products.

_____

_____   [3]

Total Marks _____ / 18

Bacterial Contamination

1 Complete this table relating to food poisoning, giving one food source and one symptom for each type of food-poisoning bacteria.

Name of Bacteria	One Food Source	One Symptom
E-Coli		
Campylobacter		
Bacillus Cereus		
Staphylococcus Aureus		

[8]

2 Explain why food-borne disease is different from food-poisoning bacteria.

....

....

....

....

....   [2]

3 Bacteria will grow if food is stored incorrectly.

Give three conditions bacteria need in order to grow.

....

....

....

....   [3]

Total Marks .... / 13

Buying and Storing Food

1 Explain the importance of storing high-risk foods correctly.

....

....

....

....

....

....

....

....

.... [4]

2 Give two food safety rules that must be followed when storing fresh fish.

Explain why each rule is needed.

Food Safety Rule	Explanation

[4]

3 If warm food is put into a refrigerator, the temperature inside the fridge will rise. What temperature range is classed as the danger zone in the fridge?
Tick the correct answer.

a) 1–4°C ☐

b) 10–72°C ☐

c) 8–13°C ☐

d) 5–63°C ☐

[1]

Total Marks .... / 9

Preparing and Cooking Food

1 State four personal hygiene rules that must be followed by people when preparing and cooking food.

....

....

....

....

.... **[4]**

....

2 Care must be taken when preparing and cooking high-risk foods. Give three examples of high-risk foods.

....

....

.... **[3]**

....

3 It is important to prepare and cook food at the correct temperature.

Name one piece of equipment used to check the temperature of a joint of meat whilst it is being cooked.

.... **[1]**

....

4 Keeping food hot for serving is important for food safety. What is the correct temperature a chicken curry must be kept at in a school canteen?

Tick the correct answer.

a) 30°C ☐

b) 45°C ☐

c) 63°C ☐

d) 90°C ☐ **[1]**

Total Marks .... / 9

Food Choices

Video Solution   Question 7

1 What is the only type of meat allowed in Judaism?

.... [1]

2 An allergy to nuts could cause what reaction? Underline the correct answer.

Fainting   **Anaphylaxis**   **Itchy scalp**   **Nose bleed**   [1]

3 Explain what Coeliac disease is.

....

....

.... [3]

4 What is the name of the condition that occurs when someone cannot digest the sugars found in milk and milk products?

.... [1]

5 What do you understand by this symbol?

....

.... [1]

6 Complete the table.

Religion	Dietary Restriction
	No pork, only Halal meat
	No beef or beef products
	No particular dietary restrictions

[3]

7 Explain the differences between Type 1 and Type 2 diabetes.

....

....

.... [3]

Total Marks .... / 13

British and International Cuisines

1 Tick one answer. 'Cuisine' relates to:

a) The way in which food is cooked in a kitchen. ☐

b) The range of dishes and foods of a particular country or region. ☐

c) The information listed on a food label. ☐

[1]

2 Which British cheese originates from Somerset? Circle the correct answer.

Stilton   **Cheddar**   **Double Gloucester**   **Red Leicester**

[1]

3 Traditional dishes are important in any society as they originate from the ingredients grown in that country or region, the local climate and traditions.

Write the dishes below next to the correct country in the table and describe the key ingredients and flavours of the dish.

Tortilla   **Cornish pasty**   **Minestrone**   **Bouillabaisse**

Shepherd's pie   **Lasagne**   **Paella**   **Tarte tatin**

Country	Dish	Key Ingredients and Flavours	
England			[4]
France			[4]
Spain			[4]
Italy			[4]

Total Marks _____ / 18

Sensory Evaluation

1 Complete the following sentence using the words below.

| together | five | evaluate | like | eat | analysis |

Sensory _____ involves using our _____ senses to

_____ how much we _____ a dish. We use these senses

_____ when we _____ our food.   [6]

2 When tasting food, what are the five basic senses?

_____

_____   [5]

3 Describe how to set up a tasting area to trial your practical work in the food room.

_____

_____

_____

_____

_____

_____   [6]

4 What do you understand by a 'triangle test'?

_____

_____

_____   [4]

5 What does a preference test aim to find out? Tick the correct answer.

   a) The sensory characteristics of a food product. ☐

   b) Whether consumers like or dislike a food product. ☐

   c) If any differences occur between two products. ☐

   d) The dominance of a sensory feature, such as crunchiness. ☐   [1]

Total Marks _____ / 22

1 Which food label indicates that the food should no longer be offered for sale in a shop? Tick the correct answer.

a) Use by ☐

b) Best before ☐

c) Display until ☐

d) Sell by ☐

[1]

2 What does GDA stand for?

_____ [1]

3 How are ingredients listed on a food label?

_____ [1]

4 Other than the ingredients, what other information must legally be present on a food label? Give six examples.

_____

_____

_____

_____

_____

_____ [6]

5 Explain how the 14 identified allergens must be displayed on a food label.

_____

_____

_____ [2]

Total Marks _____ / 11

Factors Affecting Food Choice

1 Fill in the missing words to complete the sentence.

Our enjoyment of food is affected by what the food l_____, s_____

and t_____ like. [3]

2 Give three examples of foods that are specifically eaten at religious festivals.

_____

_____

_____ [3]

3 Give three advantages of eating locally produced foods in season.

_____

_____

_____

_____ [3]

4 Circle the correct answer.

Fresh strawberries brought in a supermarket in December are most likely to have been...

exported   **genetically modified**   **imported**   **irradiated** [1]

5 Supermarkets and food retailers can influence the food we buy. Discuss the marketing strategies they could use to influence the consumers' food choice.

_____

_____

_____

_____

_____ [3]

Total Marks _____ / 13

Food and the Environment

1 Name two dishes that use up leftover food.

_____ [2]

2 What gas does waste food give off as it decomposes in landfill? Tick the correct answer.

a) Hydrogen ☐

b) Carbon monoxide ☐

c) Methane ☐

d) Carbon dioxide ☐

[1]

3 What is sustainable food? Tick the correct answer.

a) Food that lasts longer in the fridge. ☐

b) Food that will continue to be available for many years to come. ☐

c) Food that is grown nearby. ☐

d) Food that does not need to be stored in the fridge or freezer. ☐

[1]

4 Home composting is efficient, easy and clean.

What two things are needed in order to return goodness to the soil?

_____ [2]

5 When you throw away food, you waste not only the food but also the resources – such as energy, fuel and water – that went into growing, harvesting, transporting and storing the food. Discarded food then goes on to produce gas in landfill sites.

Discuss what every person can do to prevent this food waste.

_____

_____

_____

_____

_____

_____

_____ [6]

Total Marks _____ / 12

Food Provenance and Production Methods

1 What are organic foods? Tick the correct answer.

a) Foods that have been genetically modified.

b) Foods that are grown for people who are vegan.

c) Foods that are grown reliant on natural composts and manure as fertilisers.

d) Foods that are proven to be better for us to eat.

[1]

2 Explain what hydroponic farming is.

_____

_____

_____

_____

_____

[4]

3 What concerns are there about GM (Genetically Modified) food production? Tick the correct answers.

a) It is more expensive.

b) There is a possibility of new strains of microorganisms developing.

c) It is altering and playing with nature.

d) It is less resistant to plant disease.

e) It is not monitored.

[2]

4 In the food chain, name five people who have responsibility for food safety.

_____

_____

[5]

5 After the Second World War, intensive farming became popular as farmers were offered subsidies to farm large scale, low cost products.
Give three effects that this policy has had on the food chain.

_____

_____

_____

_____

[3]

Total Marks _____ / 15

Sustainability of Food

1 What does GHG stand for? Tick the correct answer.

a) Good Health Guide ☐

b) Greenhouse Gas ☐

c) Growing High Greens ☐

d) Government Health Group ☐

[1]

2 Livestock, especially cows, produce methane gas which is 20 times more harmful than CO_2.
True or false?

[1]

....

3 a) What does Fairtrade mean?

....

....

....

[2]

b) Give two examples of foods that could display this logo.

....

[1]

4 What are the advantages of buying a pack of pork chops that displays the Red Tractor logo and the British Flag?

....

....

....

....

....

....

....

....

[8]

....

Total Marks _____ / 13

1 What is condensed milk?

....

.... [1]

2 After the fat is removed from milk, it is used to make cream.
Name three different types of cream.

....

.... [3]

3 a) Name three regional varieties of cheese from the UK.

.... [3]

b) Name three French cheeses.

.... [3]

4 What is the name of the wheat used to make pasta flour?

.... [1]

5 a) What is the name of the outer layer of a grain of wheat?

.... [1]

b) When this is removed, what kind of flour is produced?

.... [1]

6 In the UK we drink mainly milk from cows, but it can also come from a variety of plant sources.
Explain why some groups of people may choose to drink plant-based milk and give some
examples of sources of this milk.

....

....

....

....

.... [4]

Total Marks .... / 17

1 Name four different methods of drying foods to preserve them.

....

.... [4]

2 a) When milk is UHT treated, what does this mean?

....

.... [2]

b) What do the letters UHT stand for?

.... [1]

c) When milk is UHT treated, what changes occur?

....

.... [3]

3 Fruits and vegetables that are transported to this country from abroad are often irradiated.

a) What does irradiated mean?

....

.... [2]

b) What changes to vitamin content may this cause?

....

.... [4]

c) Does this affect the sensory attributes of the foods?

....

.... [2]

Total Marks .... / 18

Collins

GCSE
Food Preparation And Nutrition

Practice Paper 1

Materials

Time allowed: 1 hour 45 minutes

For this paper you must have:

- a black pen
- a pencil.

Instructions

- Use black ink or black ball-point pen.
- Answer **all** questions.
- You must answer the questions in the spaces provided. Do not write outside the box around each page or on blank pages.
- Do all rough work in this answer book. Cross through any work you do not want to be marked.

Information

- The marks for questions are shown in brackets.
- The maximum mark for this paper is 100.
- You are reminded of the need for good English and clear presentation in your answers.

Name: ....

Practice Exam Paper 1

Section A consists of multiple choice questions.

There are 20 marks available.
Answer all questions.

For each question you should shade in **one** box.

An example is shown below.

Which food is high in fat?

    A Bread ⬜

    B Cheese ⬛

    C Broccoli ⬜

    D Apple ⬜

Question 1 is about diet, nutrition and health.

0 1 . 1 Citrus fruits are an excellent source of:

A Calcium ◯

B Vitamin C ◯

C Vitamin B ◯

D Calories ◯ **[1 mark]**

0 1 . 2 Which vitamin is needed to help prevent a birth defect called Spina bifida?

A Vitamin D ◯

B Vitamin A ◯

C Folic acid ◯

D Vitamin E ◯ **[1 mark]**

0 1 . 3 Retinol is an alternative name for which vitamin?

A Vitamin A ◯

B Vitamin C ◯

C Vitamin B2 ◯

D Vitamin K ◯ **[1 mark]**

0 1 . 4 What is the name of the medical condition, common in elderly people, when bones become weak, brittle and break easily?

A Anaemia ◯

B Angina ◯

C Osteoporosis ◯

D Diabetes ◯ **[1 mark]**

Practice Exam Paper 1

Question 2 is about food safety.

0 2 · 1 What is the temperature range regarded as the danger zone?

    A −10°C–20°C ⬜

    B 0°C–70°C ⬜

    C 5°C–63°C ⬜

    D 5°C–45°C ⬜ **[1 mark]**

0 2 · 2 Which one of the following is the primary cause of food-borne illness in the UK and most often associated with undercooked chicken?

    A Bacillus cereus ⬜

    B Listeria ⬜

    C E-Coli ⬜

    D Campylobacter jejuni ⬜ **[1 mark]**

0 2 · 3 Which one of the following does bacteria need in order to multiply?

    A Acid ⬜

    B Cold ⬜

    C Moisture ⬜

    D Salt ⬜ **[1 mark]**

0 2 · 4 Which one of the following statements is true? Food is cooked to:

    A make it easier to eat after cooking. ⬜

    B change the appearance of the food. ⬜

    C make it safe to eat. ⬜

    D combine proteins, fats and carbohydrates. ⬜ **[1 mark]**

Question 3 is about food science.

`0 3`·`1` What causes the ripening and browning of bananas?

A   Enzyme activity ◯

B   Pathogens ◯

C   Sensory factors ◯

D   Contamination ◯   [1 mark]

`0 3`·`2` What happens to fish flesh proteins during cooking?

A   Proteins are gelatinised. ◯

B   Proteins are denatured by heat. ◯

C   Proteins are homogenised. ◯

D   Proteins are rehydrated. ◯   [1 mark]

`0 3`·`3` Béchamel sauce needs a flavoured milk. How is flavour imparted into the milk?

A   It is agitated. ◯

B   It is poached. ◯

C   It is stewed. ◯

D   It is infused. ◯   [1 mark]

`0 3`·`4` A sauce recipe lists flour, milk and fat. What is the role of the flour?

A   Thickener ◯

B   Flavouring ◯

C   Colour ◯

D   Enriching ◯   [1 mark]

Practice Exam Paper 1

Question 4 is about food provenance.

`0 4 · 1` What are food miles?

    A The distance to the takeaway from your home. ⬭

    B The distance that you travel to get to the local supermarket. ⬭

    C The distance that food travels from its point of origin to your table. ⬭

    D The distance that food travels from its point of origin to the supermarket. ⬭ **[1 mark]**

`0 4 · 2` What is free-range farming?

    A A farm using large fields with no hedgerows or fencing. ⬭

    B A farm where animals live in huge barns for their entire life. ⬭

    C A farm where animals can access outdoor areas for part of their life. ⬭

    D A farm where animals can access outdoor areas for their entire life. ⬭ **[1 mark]**

`0 4 · 3` Cream is a by-product of milk. Which of the following types of cream is most suitable for piping?

    A Double ⬭

    B Single ⬭

    C Crème fraiche ⬭

    D Sour cream ⬭ **[1 mark]**

`0 4 · 4` Canning is a common method for high temperature storage of milk. Which milk is bought in cans?

    A Sterilised ⬭

    B Condensed ⬭

    C Pasteurised ⬭

    D Ultra-Heat Treated (UHT) ⬭ **[1 mark]**

Question 5 is about food choices.

0 5 · 1 Current Healthy Eating Guidelines recommend that we should eat how many portions of fruit and vegetables every day?

A 3–5 ⬜

B 4–6 ⬜

C 5–7 ⬜

D 6–8 ⬜ **[1 mark]**

0 5 · 2 Which section do potatoes belong to on the Eatwell Guide?

A Blue – dairy and alternatives. ⬜

B Green – fruit and vegetables. ⬜

C Purple – oils and spreads. ⬜

D Yellow – starchy carbohydrates. ⬜ **[1 mark]**

0 5 · 3 Which of the following foods is high in dietary fibre?

A Wholemeal bread ⬜

B Chicken ⬜

C Eggs ⬜

D Tomato ketchup ⬜ **[1 mark]**

0 5 · 4 Type 1 diabetes is a condition in which:

A the pancreas makes too much glycogen. ⬜

B the stomach cannot digest sugar. ⬜

C the pancreas makes too much insulin. ⬜

D the pancreas makes no insulin. ⬜ **[1 mark]**

Practice Exam Paper 1

Section B

Answer all questions in this section.
There are 80 marks available.

Question 6 is about diet, nutrition and health.

0 6 · 1 Give four reasons why it is important to follow the guidance of the Eatwell Guide.

....

....

....

....

[4 marks]

0 6 · 2 State three reasons why someone may not be able to follow the guidance of the Eatwell Guide.

....

....

....

[3 marks]

06 . 3 Explain the dietary advice you would give to women to ensure a healthy pregnancy and healthy newborn baby.

_____

_____

_____

_____

_____

_____

_____

_____

_____

_____

[10 marks]

Practice Exam Paper 1

Question 7 is about carbohydrates and food preparation.

0 7 . 1 Discuss the reasons for cooking and the changes brought about by boiling potatoes, rice and dried pasta.

....

....

....

....

[4 marks]

0 7 . 2 Compare the two sauce recipes below and explain which would make the best sauce to pour and flow over a pudding.

Sauce A	250ml milk, 15g fat, 15g flour
Sauce B	250ml milk, 30g fat, 30g flour

....

....

....

[3 marks]

0 7 . 3 On the chart provided, show how Sauce A would be different to Sauce B when tested for viscosity.

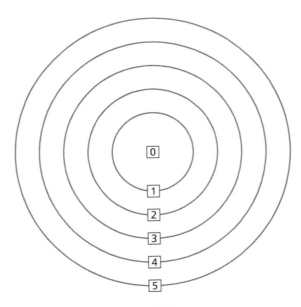

[2 marks]

0 7 · 4 Potatoes needed for making fishcakes are prepared according to the steps in the chart below. State the reasons for each of the stages. One has been completed for you.

Preparation and Cooking Stages	Reasons
Peel old potatoes.	*To remove dirt and skin to speed up cooking.*
Chop potatoes.	
Boil potatoes.	
Mash cooked potatoes.	

[3 marks]

0 7 · 5 Explain scientifically how the texture of mashed potato spread over the surface of fish pie could be changed by grilling.

....

....

[3 marks]

Practice Exam Paper 1

Question 8 is about food safety and food labelling.

0 8 · 1 Legally, food products must have the name of the product printed on the label.
State six other items of information that must be given by law.

....

....

....

....

....

....

[6 marks]

0 8 · 2 Consumers use information from the labels of food products when choosing what
to buy.

Here are some ingredients used in a ready-made quiche.

> Ingredients:
>
> 100g plain flour, 60g chopped onion, 125ml egg, 75g grated cheese,
> 50g butter, 73ml water, 150ml milk, 10g chopped parsley

How would they appear on an ingredients list?

....

....

....

[6 marks]

0 8 · 3 Why is it important to include the manufacturer's name and address on the label?

....

[1 mark]

Question 9 is about sensory evaluation.

| 0 | 9 | . | 1 | Give two reasons why sensory evaluation is carried out by food manufacturers.

....

....

....

[2 marks]

| 0 | 9 | . | 2 | Explain why testers should have a glass of water when they are tasting food products.

....

....

[1 mark]

| 0 | 9 | . | 3 | Describe how you would carry out a sensory analysis test to compare a cook-chill cottage pie and a homemade cottage pie.

....

....

....

....

....

[4 marks]

Practice Exam Paper 1

Question 10 is about cooking food, heat transfer and selecting appropriate cooking methods.

Here is a recipe list for a pasta bake.

Dried fusilli pasta

Homemade roux sauce

Grated cheddar cheese with breadcrumbs

Oven-roasted vegetables

`1 0 . 1` Which cooking method would you select to cook the pasta and why?

....

....

....

[3 marks]

`1 0 . 2` Give three reasons why it is important to stir a flour-based roux sauce when cooking it.

....

....

....

[3 marks]

`1 0 . 3` Which heat transfer method would be most appropriate to ensure the top of the pasta bake is golden brown and crisp?

....

....

[2 marks]

1 0 · 4 Explain what is meant by oven-roasted vegetables and discuss the different characteristics they would have compared with boiled vegetables.

....

....

....

....

[4 marks]

Practice Exam Paper 1

Question 11 is about provenance and sustainability.

Food miles are the distance that our food travels from its point of origin to your table.

1 1 . 1 Suggest two ways that we can reduce food miles.

_____

_____

_____

[2 marks]

1 1 . 2 Discuss why we are concerned about the distance our food has travelled before it is cooked and eaten.

_____

_____

_____

_____

[4 marks]

Question 12 is about provenance and sustainability.

1 2 . 1 All food must be traceable from field to fork.

Just before Easter 2022, a brand of chocolate eggs were discovered to possibly contain salmonella. Some batches had a recall notice issued.

What regulations are in place for manufacturers and the Food Standards Agency to ensure that recalls don't happen and that foods are safe?

....

....

....

....

....

....

....

....

....

....

[10 marks]

END OF QUESTIONS

Collins

GCSE
Food Preparation And Nutrition

Practice Paper 2

Materials

Time allowed: 1 hour 45 minutes

For this paper you must have:

- a black pen
- a pencil.

Instructions

- Use black ink or black ball-point pen.
- Answer **all** questions.
- You must answer the questions in the spaces provided. Do not write outside the box around each page or on blank pages.
- Do all rough work in this answer book. Cross through any work you do not want to be marked.

Information

- The marks for questions are shown in brackets.
- The maximum mark for this paper is 100.
- You are reminded of the need for good English and clear presentation in your answers.

Name: _____

Section A consists of multiple choice questions.

There are 20 marks available.
Answer all questions.

For each question you should shade in **one** box.

An example is shown below.

Which food is high in fat?

    A Bread   ⬜

    B Cheese   ⬛

    C Broccoli   ⬜

    D Apple   ⬜

Practice Exam Paper 2

Question 1 is about diet, nutrition and health.

0 1 · 1 Which mineral element is needed by the body to assist with the absorption of Vitamin C?

    A Fluoride   ◯

    B Calcium   ◯

    C Phosphorous   ◯

    D Iron   ◯   **[1 mark]**

0 1 · 2 High blood pressure can be linked to a diet high in:

    A Sugar   ◯

    B Protein   ◯

    C Calcium   ◯

    D Salt   ◯   **[1 mark]**

0 1 · 3 A deficiency of vitamin B12 is linked to which condition?

    A Heart disease   ◯

    B Pernicious anaemia   ◯

    C Spina bifida   ◯

    D Stroke   ◯   **[1 mark]**

0 1 · 4 Folate (folic acid) is needed both before and during early pregnancy for the development of what in the foetus?

    A Strong bones   ◯

    B The neural tube   ◯

    C The liver   ◯

    D Blood   ◯   **[1 mark]**

Question 2 is about food safety.

0 2 · 1 Food poisoning is most likely to occur if:

    A cooked meat is stored in the refrigerator.   ◯

    B cold cooked meat is stored in the freezer.   ◯

    C food is stored above 63°C for no more than two hours.   ◯

    D cooked meat is kept at room temperature.   ◯   **[1 mark]**

0 2 · 2 Ambient food storage areas should be:

    A warm, dark and pest-proof.   ◯

    B damp, cool and well ventilated.   ◯

    C light, warm and secure.   ◯

    D dry, cool and well ventilated.   ◯   **[1 mark]**

0 2 · 3 If cooked food is not chilled quickly:

    A viruses will produce toxins.   ◯

    B moulds will begin to grow.   ◯

    C bacteria will start to multiply.   ◯

    D allergens will be created.   ◯   **[1 mark]**

0 2 · 4 Which colour board should raw chicken be prepared upon?

    A Blue   ◯

    B Brown   ◯

    C Red   ◯

    D Green   ◯   **[1 mark]**

Practice Exam Paper 2

Question 3 is about food science.

0 3 · 1 Which type of sugar is most effective when aerating a cream cake mixture?

    A Demerara sugar   ◯

    B Caster sugar   ◯

    C Icing sugar   ◯

    D Dark molasses   ◯   **[1 mark]**

0 3 · 2 Eggs are cooked in a soufflé. How does heat change the raw egg proteins?

    A The eggs are gelatinised.   ◯

    B The eggs are fermented.   ◯

    C The eggs are coagulated.   ◯

    D The eggs are melted.   ◯   **[1 mark]**

0 3 · 3 Which heat transfer method is most likely to bring about dextrinisation?

    A Microwave rays   ◯

    B Convection currents   ◯

    C Conduction   ◯

    D Radiated heat   ◯   **[1 mark]**

0 3 · 4 When a blow torch is used on the surface of a crème brûlée, how is the sugar affected?

    A It is condensed.   ◯

    B It is coagulated.   ◯

    C It is caramelised.   ◯

    D It is curdled.   ◯   **[1 mark]**

Question 4 is about food provenance.

`0 4`·`1` Which of the following is a way of reducing food waste?

    A FIFO (Fridge Intensive Food Organisation) ◯

    B FIFO (Food In Fridge Organisation) ◯

    C FIFO (First In First Out) ◯

    D FIFO (Food In Foil Opened) ◯ **[1 mark]**

`0 4`·`2` What is hydroponic farming?

    A Fish farms which allow newly hatched young to mature before releasing them into the wild. ◯

    B Farms where fruits and vegetables are grown using large irrigation channels. ◯

    C Farms where fruit and vegetables are grown using large spray-armed sprinkler systems. ◯

    D Fruits and vegetables grown in large polytunnels using nutrient-rich liquids rather than soil. ◯ **[1 mark]**

`0 4`·`3` MSC is an international non-profit organisation with a mission to stop overfishing. What does MSC stand for?

    A More Sustainable Catches ◯

    B Marine Sourced Cod ◯

    C Marine Sustainable Catches ◯

    D Marine Stewardship Council ◯ **[1 mark]**

`0 4`·`4` What is the primary process that turns wheat into flour called?

    A Crushing ◯

    B Milling ◯

    C Grinding ◯

    D Rolling ◯ **[1 mark]**

Practice Exam Paper 2

Question 5 is about food choices.

0 5 · 1 People who have an adverse reaction to gluten are described as:

    A diabetic ◯

    B lactose intolerant ◯

    C anaemic ◯

    D coeliac ◯ **[1 mark]**

0 5 · 2 Salt in the diet can be linked to high blood pressure. What is the recommended amount per day for adults?

    A No more than 10g. ◯

    B No more than 12g. ◯

    C No more than 6g. ◯

    D No more than 8g. ◯ **[1 mark]**

0 5 · 3 A baby is born with a supply of iron in which organ of the body?

    A Liver ◯

    B Kidneys ◯

    C Spleen ◯

    D Blood ◯ **[1 mark]**

0 5 · 4 Which of the following is NOT a type of carbohydrate?

    A Starch ◯

    B Sucrose ◯

    C Glycogen ◯

    D Cholesterol ◯ **[1 mark]**

Section B

Answer all questions in this section.
There are 80 marks available.

Question 6 is about diet, nutrition and health.

0 6 . 1 Kiwi fruit is a good source of vitamin C, which could be included in a fresh fruit salad. Name two other good sources of vitamin C that could be included in a fresh fruit salad.

_____

[2 marks]

0 6 . 2 State four reasons why the body requires vitamin C.

_____

_____

_____

_____

[4 marks]

0 6 . 3 Vitamin C is a water-soluble vitamin that is easily lost in food preparation. Give four ways to help prevent the loss of vitamin C.

_____

_____

_____

_____

[4 marks]

0 6 . 4 Discuss the advantages and disadvantages of buying fruits and vegetables grown in the UK.

....

....

....

....

....

....

....

[6 marks]

Question 7 is about functional and chemical properties of protein.

0 7 . 1 Explain how using an electric whisk to make meringue changes the protein structure of egg white. You may use diagrams to support your answer.

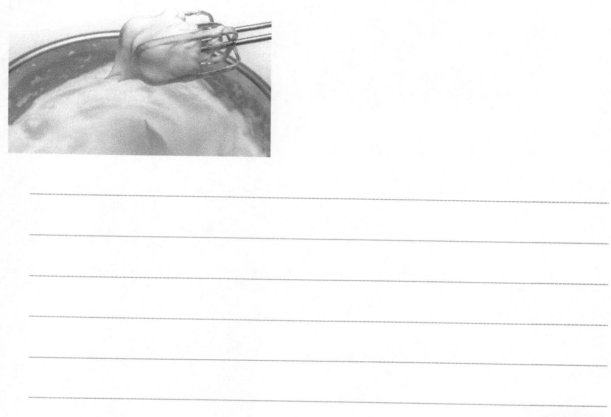

....

....

....

....

....

[4 marks]

0 7 . 2 Explain the scientific reasons for the changes that occur when eggs are boiled.

....

....

....

....

....

....

[6 marks]

0 7 . 3 Explain why milk curdles when lemon juice is added.

....

....

....

....

....

....

[6 marks]

Question 8 is about cooking food, heat transfer and selecting appropriate cooking methods.

0 8 · 1 Describe how heat transfer methods work when boiling potatoes on the hob.

....

[2 marks]

0 8 · 2 Steaming is classed as a water-based method of cooking. Name two other classifications of cooking methods, giving an example for each of a dish or recipe cooked in that way.

....

....

[4 marks]

0 8 · 3 State two health benefits from choosing to steam vegetables.

....

....

[2 marks]

0 8 · 4 Using data from the chart below, explain how cooking methods affect the nutritional outcome of potatoes cooked in different ways.

Potatoes cooked in different ways	Vitamin C content per 100g portion	Fat content per 100g portion
Potatoes boiled in water	6 mg	0.1 g
Oven chips baked	12 mg	4.9 g
Potato crisps	35 mg	28.8 mg

Source: Manual of Nutrition 12th edition

....

....

....

....

....

[6 marks]

Question 9 is about food safety.

`0 9` · `1` 'High-risk foods are most likely to cause food poisoning.'

Explain this statement.

_____

_____

_____

_____

_____

_____

[6 marks]

`0 9` · `2` Explain how a temperature probe should be used correctly on a cooked chicken.

_____

_____

_____

_____

[4 marks]

Practice Exam Paper 2

Question 10 is about food production.

1 0 . 1 Name two types of milk that have been processed to have a longer shelf life than fresh milk.

....

[2 marks]

1 0 . 2 Explain the differences between skimmed and semi-skimmed milk.

....

....

[2 marks]

The picture shows a refrigerator stocked with alternatives to cows' milk.

1 0 . 3 Give four examples of what these products can be made from.

....

....

[4 marks]

`1` `0` · `4` Explain why cows' milk alternatives have become very popular in the last few years.

....

....

....

....

....

[4 marks]

Practice Exam Paper 2

Question 11 is about provenance and sustainability.

11·1 Explain what is meant by free-range farming.

....

....

[1 mark]

11·2 What are the benefits of free-range farming?

....

....

....

[3 marks]

11·3 Give two examples of free-range products.

....

[2 marks]

11·4 Explain what it means if chicken has a label which says it has been 'barn reared'.

....

....

....

....

[3 marks]

11·5 Explain how organic vegetables and fruits are grown.

....

....

....

[3 marks]

END OF QUESTIONS

Answers

Food Preparation Skills – pages 4–8

Page 4 Knife Skills

1. c) ✓ [1]
2. d) ✓ [1]
3. **Three from: Safety Rule:** A flat and stable surface should be used for cutting [1] **Reason:** to prevent slipping and movement/injury. [1] **Safety Rule:** Keep knives sharp and clean [1] **Reason:** a blunt knife is more likely to cause a cut because more pressure needs to be applied to use it to cut. [1] **Safety Rule:** Keep knife handles grease-free [1] **Reason:** so that they do not slip and cause injury. [1] **Safety Rule:** Hold the point downwards when carrying a knife [1] **Reason:** to protect others in the room. [1] **Safety Rule:** Do not put knives in the washing-up bowl [1] **Reason:** someone may put their hand in the bowl and sustain a cut [1] **Safety Rule:** Do not leave a knife on the edge of a table or chopping board [1] **Reason:** this can fall and cause injury. [1]
4. **Name of knife hold 1:** Bridge hold [1] **Explanation:** Form a bridge with thumb and index finger, hold item flat side down on chopping board, position knife under the bridge and cut firmly downwards. [1] **Name of knife hold 2:** Claw grip [1] **Explanation:** Place item to be cut flat side down on chopping board, shape hand into a claw, tuck thumb inside fingers, rest the claw on item to be sliced, use other hand to slice the item, moving clawed fingers away as cutting progresses. [1]

Page 5 Fish

1. c) ✓ [1]
2. d) ✓ [1]
3. Fish cooks quickly because the **muscle** [1] is short and the **connective tissue** [1] is thin. The connective tissue is made up of **collagen** [1] and will change into **gelatine** [1] and **coagulate** [1] at 60 °C [1].
4. a) Flat fish [1]
   b) **Any flat fish, e.g.** Plaice; Sole; Halibut [1]
   c) Filleting knife [1]
   d) Blue [1]
   e) Use a filleting knife to descale and remove the fins. Cut off the head just behind the gills. [1] Cut from head to tail down to the bone, to one side of the centre line. [1] Turn the knife almost parallel to the table. Make a long, smooth cut horizontally against the backbone towards the outer edge. Separate the fillet from the bone and remove it. [1]

Page 6 Meat

1. d) ✓ [1]
2. c) ✓ [1]
3. Muscles that work a lot, such as the thighs and shoulders of animals, give tough meat, e.g. shin beef, brisket. [1] Cuts of meat from muscle areas that do a lot of work will need longer, slower cooking methods in wet heat, e.g. stewing, braising, pot roasting and casseroling. [1] Meat from tougher cuts can be ground or minced to break up the connective tissues so that it cooks more quickly. [1]
4. Red [1]
5. **Any two of:** Using a marinade [1]; Mincing [1]; Using a steak hammer [1]
6. The **browning** [1] of meat is caused by a reaction with natural **sugars** [1] and proteins to produce a dark colour. This occurrence is called the **Maillard** [1] reaction or non-enzymic browning. As the meat cooks, the proteins **coagulate** [1] and produce a firm texture. Collagen is broken down into **gelatine** [1].

Page 7 Prepare, Combine and Shape

1. a) ✓ [1]
2. Folding and stirring are methods used to **combine** [1] and **mix** [1] ingredients. Folding is different to stirring because it is a careful **figure-of-eight** [1] movement used for adding flour when **cake** [1] making. Folding **retains** [1] air in a cake mixture helping the cooked cake to have a light airy **texture** [1].
3. a) Rolling pin [1]
   b) Roll [1] and fold [1]
   c) Piping bag [1]; Star nozzle [1]
   d) Portion [1], roll [1] and tie by hand [1]

Page 8 Dough

1. a) By using a pasta machine (or rolling pin). [1]
   b) The texture changes [1] to hard and dry. [1]
2. b) ✓ [1]
3. **Any two valid ingredients with correct colours achieved for [4], e.g.** Beetroot powder [1] – purple [1]; Spinach powder [1] – green [1]; Tomato puree [1] – red [1]; Squid ink [1] – black [1]
4. Pastry; Bread; Pasta **circled** [3]
5. The fat is melted [1], the water and fat are heated to a rolling boil [1] then mixed into the flour.
6. True [1]

Food Nutrition and Health – pages 9–14

Page 9 Protein and Fat

1. amino acids [2]
2. a) **Any three from:** Soya; Nuts; Seeds; Pulses (lentils, kidney beans etc.); Mycoprotein (Quorn); TVP (Texturised Vegetable protein) [3]
   b) Cauliflower cheese; Mushroom and Lentil Bake **circled**. [2]
3. When proteins of low biological value (LBV) are eaten together to provide all essential amino acids. [1] **Examples:** beans on toast, lentil soup and bread, hummus and pitta bread etc. [1]
4. fatty acids [1] glycerol [1]
5. c) ✓ [1]
6. **Any three suitable answers, e.g.** Oily fish; Nuts; Seeds; Avocados; Vegetable oils; Soya beans; Some functional food such as yoghurts and spreads (e.g. Activia, Benecol) [3]

Page 10 Carbohydrate

1. energy [1]
2. Photosynthesis [1]
3. Constipation is when faeces become difficult to expel from the body [1] because they are hard and small. [1]
4. c) ✓ [1]
5. Monosaccharides, Disaccharides, Polysaccharides [3]
6. Starches have to be digested into sugars [1] before they can be absorbed into the bloodstream. [1] This is slow energy release.
7. Excess carbohydrate is converted into fat and stored under the skin. [1] This is the main cause of obesity, which can be directly linked to many conditions such as heart disease, stroke, cancers and Type 2 diabetes. [1] In addition, a high consumption of sugar in the diet in the main cause of dental decay. [1]

Page 11 Vitamins

1. **Three from:** Oranges; Lemons; Limes; Grapefruit; Kiwi fruit; Blackcurrants; Potatoes; Tomatoes; Green vegetables, e.g. kale, cabbage, Brussel sprouts [3]
2. b) ✓ [1]
3. Folate (Folic acid) [1]
4. **Three from:** Prepare foods quickly just before serving; Use small amounts of boiling water to cook; Use cooking liquid to make sauces/gravy; Avoid lots of cutting of vegetables; Instead of cooking in water, steam, fry or grill. [3]
5. **Any suitable function given for each vitamin. Examples given in the table.** [5]

Vitamin	Function
Vitamin A	Normal iron metabolism; Maintenance of normal vision; Maintenance of skin and membranes; Healthy immune function
Vitamin K	Normal clotting of blood
Vitamin C	Absorption of iron; Production of collagen to bind connective tissue; Antioxidant – protects from environmental pollutants
Vitamin D	Absorption of calcium and phosphorus; Maintenance and strength of bones and teeth
Vitamin B1	Release of energy from carbohydrates; Healthy nervous system function; Normal growth in children

Page 12 Minerals and Water

1. Iron [1]
2. Iron supports the production of **haemoglobin [1]** in red blood cells, which transport **oxygen [1]** around the body.
3. a) Dehydration [1]
   b) **Any three from:** For normal brain function; To decrease risk of kidney problems; For normal blood pressure; To assist healthy bowel movements; To make body fluids – blood saliva mucus membranes; To aid milk production in lactating women. [3]
4. a) Rickets [1]
   b) Osteoporosis [1]
5. **Three from:** Red meats; Liver; Lentils; Dried apricots; Cocoa; Chocolate; Corned beef; Curry spices; Green leafy vegetables e.g. spinach; Breakfast cereals fortified with iron. [3]

Page 13 Making Informed Choices

1. Fruit and Vegetables (green); Potatoes, Bread, Rice Pasta and other starchy carbohydrates (yellow). [2]
2. For breast-fed babies, the first milk that a mother produces is called **colostrum [1]** and it is full of **antibodies. [1]**
3. Anaemia is caused by a lack of iron in the blood. After menstruation begins in puberty, [1] iron is needed in greater amounts to replace blood losses. [1]
4. Osteoporosis **underlined.** [1]
5. Pulse vegetables [1] and beans, such as lentils, soya beans, kidney beans, baked beans, chickpeas. [1]
6. Calcium [1] – The developing baby's bones require a good supply of calcium from the mother's diet. [1] Iron [1] – A pregnant woman will need an iron-rich diet to make additional blood for the baby and to lay down an iron store in the baby's liver. [1] Folate (folic acid) [1] – This is needed both before and during early

pregnancy for the development of the neural tube in the baby. This is to help prevent the condition spina bifida. [1]

Page 14 Diet, Nutrition and Health

1. Obesity [1]
2. Body Mass Index (BMI) [1]
3. Elderly people require a good supply of calcium and vitamin D in the diet to ensure maximum bone strength and help prevent the condition osteoporosis. [1] This can cause bones to become more brittle and break easily. It can also cause the spine to curve, making walking more difficult. [1]
4. Fibre/NSP [1]
5. Sugar increases acids on the teeth [1], which erode the protective enamel on the teeth causing irreparable tooth decay. [1]
6. **Any three from:** Tiredness; Lack of energy; Shortness of breath; Pale complexion [3]
7. In Type 2 **diabetes [1]** too little or no **insulin [1]** is produced in the **pancreas [1]** resulting in high levels of **sugar [1]** in the **blood. [1]**

Food Science – pages 15–19

Page 15 Cooking of Food, Heat Transfer and Selecting Appropriate Cooking Methods

1. **Oven-roasted vegetables – Any two from:** Browned; Crispy; Added fat [2] **Boiled vegetables – Any two from:** Tender/Soft; Wet; No added fat [2]
2. b) ✓ [1]
3. Radiation [1] from a grill. [1]
4. a) It tenderises the salmon [1] and makes it safe to eat. [1]
   b) Marinating adds flavour and/ or colour. [1] It tenderises the chicken. [1]
5. When making a sauce, heat is transferred from the hob through the base of the pan by **conduction [1]** and through the sauce by **convection. [1]** Stirring prevents **sticking [1]** on the base of the pan and distributes **heat [1]** to aid **thickening. [1]**

Page 16 Proteins and Enzymic Browning

1. a) Once cut, the fruit inside the skin allows oxidation/air. [1] This is enzymic browning. [1]
   b) **Any one from:** Add lemon juice; Poach them; Add a glaze [1]
2. a) It will be set. [1] It will be browned. [1]
   b) The heat [1] causes the mixture to coagulate. [1] Coagulation is a type of protein denaturation [1], which occurs when the amino acids found in the egg protein change shape after cooking. [1]
3. a) Bromelain [1]
   b) It would tenderise the prawns. [1]
4. b) ✓ [1] c) ✓ [1]
5. Gluten **circled.** [1]

Page 17 Carbohydrates

1. It softens the onions. [1] It sweetens the onions. [1] It caramelises the sugars in the onions. [1]
2. a) **Any two from:** Cornflour; Plain wheatflour; Arrowroot; Thickening granules [2]
   b) Starch gelatinises in moist heat. [1] The starch swells and thickens when boiled. [1] It needs stirring. [1]
3. **Any two from:** Texture becomes crisp/ crunchy; Flavour becomes sweeter; Colour changes to charred/golden. [2]
4. a) For heat transfer distribution [1]; For distribution of starch in the flour [1]; Smooth gelatinisation/no lumps [1]; To prevent sticking to the base of the pan. [1]
   b) ii) ✓ [1] iv) ✓ [1]

Page 18 Fats and Oils

1. To provide colour (yellowy colour) [1], to add a buttery flavour [1], shortening [1] due to preventing the development of gluten [1] in the flour dough.
2. a) **See middle column of table below.** [3]
   b) **See last column of table below. Any correct dish for each preparation method, examples given in the table.** [3]

Temperature of Fat	Food Preparation Method	Example of Dish
Chilled temperature	Rubbing-in	Shortcrust pastry
Room temperature	Creaming	Bakewell tart toppings
Warm pan temperature	Melting method	Flapjack

3. a) **Two from:** To create a light cake; To create an open/fluffy texture; So the cake rises. [2]
   b) **Any two from:** Creaming method; Whisking method; Using a food mixer [2]
4. Air-in-fat [1]

Page 19 Raising Agents

1. a) **Any two suitable recipes/products [2] with appropriate mechanical method of trapping air [2]. Examples given in the table.** [4]

Recipe/Product Name	Mechanical (Physical) Method to Trap Air
Puff pastry	Folding/Layering
Cakes	Sieving flour/Beating
Cream	Whipping to thicken
Swiss roll	Whisking

   b) Chemical [1], **Example:** Baking powder/Self-raising flour/ Bicarbonate of soda/Cream of tartar [1] **OR** Biological [1], **Example:** Yeast [1]

2.

Product	Raising Agent
Victoria Sandwich	S.R. flour [1]
Muffins	Baking powder [1]
English pancakes	Beating [1]
Choux buns	Steam production [1]

3. Bicarbonate of soda **[1]**
4. Gas-in-liquid foam **[1]**
5. A ready-mix raising agent [1] in the correct proportion [1] of cream of tartar [1] and bicarbonate of soda. [1]

Food Safety – pages 20–24

Page 20 Microorganisms, Enzymes and Food Spoilage

1. **Two from:** Bacteria; Yeast; Mould; Fungi/fungus **[2]**
2. **Three from:** Food; Temperature/ warmth; Moisture/liquid; pH value; Time; HBV protein content; Oxygen/ air; Carbon dioxide (Do **not** accept a named method of preservation). **[3]**
3. **Three from:** Change in colour/ discolouration; Change in size/it shrinks; Change in texture/soft/dry/ slimy; Change in consistency; Mould; Unpleasant smell; Unpleasant taste. **[3]**
4. **Three from:** Make sure storage containers are clean; Store dry foods in airtight containers/sealed packets; Store in a cool, dry place; Wash shelves regularly/deal with spills; Do not top up existing stock with new; Check storage times/best before dates; Cupboards should be free from vermin and pests.**[3]**
5. **Two from:** Add lemon juice to fruit to prevent browning; Blanche vegetables before freezing; Immerse potatoes in water to prevent discolouration; Refridgerate or freeze; Dehydrate **[2]**

Page 21 Microorganisms in Food Production

1. Bacteria are **single**-celled [1] organisms which are able to reproduce **rapidly.** [1] Some are **harmful** [1] and cause **food poisoning** [1] or even death. Some are harmless and used in **cheese**-making. [1] **Probiotic** [1] bacteria help **digestion.** [1]
2. a) In blue-veined cheeses, e.g. Stilton, Danish blue, harmless moulds are used to produce specific flavours, textures and aromas. [1] Some sausages, such as salami, incorporate starter cultures of moulds to improve flavour and reduce bacterial spoilage during curing. [1] Microbial rennet is used for making vegetarian and other cheeses. [1] Mould can improve the appearance of foods. [1]
   b) Cheese and yoghurt manufacture uses cultures of lactic acid bacteria [1] to produce characteristic flavours and textures to these products. [1] Fermented foods e.g. Sauerkraut: bacteria will improve flavour and texture [1] and have a positive effect on the bacteria flora of the digestive gut. [1]

3. **Three from:** Pepperoni; Chorizo; Salami; Dried ham **[3]**

Page 22 Bacterial Contamination

1.

Name of Bacteria	One Food Source	One Symptom
E-Coli	**One from:** Raw meat; Untreated milk; Water [1]	**One from:** Vomiting; Blood in diar- rhoea; Kidney damage or failure; Gastroenteritis in humans [1]
Campylobacter	**One from:** Meat; Shellfish; Untreated water; Washing raw poultry [1]	**One from:** Diarrhoea; Headache; Fever; Abdominal pain (**Do not accept** vomiting) [1]
Bacillus Cereus	**One from:** Cooked rice; Herbs and spices; Starchy food products [1]	**One from:** Nausea; Vomiting; Diarrhoea [1]
Staphylococcus Aureus	**One from:** Anything touched by dirty hands; Cooked sliced meats; Dairy products [1]	**One from:** Vomiting; Diarrhoea; Abdominal pain [1]

2. Food-poisoning bacteria is caused by bacteria multiplying in or on food products. [1] Food-borne disease is caused by pathogens carried on food – they do not multiply on the food but in a person who has eaten the food. **[1]**
3. **Three from:** Moisture/moist/damp; Oxygen; Time; Warmth/warm; Food **[3]**

Page 23 Buying and Storing Food

1. **Answers could include the following points for a maximum of [4]. Answers must relate to food handling and storage:** Food poisoning occurs when foods spoil rapidly [1] because of a high-water content and high nutritional content. [1] Because of warm, moist conditions [1] food poisoning would occur in **any named high-risk food [1] (e.g.** raw and cooked meat, poultry and fish, cheese, milk and dairy products, eggs and cooked rice). Food deteriorates rapidly making it unsafe [1] to eat because of microorganism/enzyme/natural decay activity. [1] When using highly perishable food, handlers must check date marks [1] so that safety of handled products is ensured due to their short shelf life. [1] Cross-contamination [1] will occur if high risk foods are exposed to poor hygiene or storage: **any of the named following examples:** food to food (raw/cooked/ pre purchased)/ Personal or kitchen hygiene/Food handler to food/Equipment to food/ Pest to food/Pet to food. [1] Store at correct temperatures/out of the danger zone. **[1]**

2. **Any two rules from the following [2] with correct explanation as shown below [2]:**

Food Safety Rule	Explanation
• Store correctly as soon as possible.	• To slow down microbial growth/ deterioration/ spoilage.
• Do not leave at room tem- perature/in the danger zone.	• Bacteria multiply more rapidly at warm tempera- tures; Bacteria multiply rapidly between 5°C and 63°C/danger zone; Bacteria multiply every 20 minutes.
• Store at 0 to below 5°C; Store in the re- frigerator, NOT on lower shelf; Store in the freezer –18°C.	• Bacteria multiply slowly in cold tem- peratures; Bacteria are dormant in the freezer; To prevent pathogen- ic bacteria multi- plying they must be stored below 5°C; Fish should be not stored in the danger zone (5–63°C).
• Cover in airtight container.	• Covering prevents cross contamina- tion.
• Use by the use- by date.	• Use-by dates indicate when the food is still safe to eat.
• Use oldest food first; Label clearly with date.	• Allows for stock rotation; First in first out (FIFO).
• Check internal temperature of the refrigerator.	• The refrigerator must be working correctly and be well maintained.

3. d) ✓ **[1]**

Page 24 Preparing and Cooking Food

1. **Four from:** Tie back hair; Cover long hair/beards with hair nets; Do not cough, spit, pick nose or sneeze over foods; Do not chew when serving food; Do not put fingers into food being served; Use clean teaspoon each time for tasting foods; Do not double dip when tasting food; Wear protective clothing, e.g. clean apron; Wear disposable gloves when handling food; Wash hands before serving food; Wash hands after using the toilet, on return from outside and after handling raw foods; Keep fingernails short and clean; Do not wear nail varnish or false nails; Do not allow sweat to go onto food; Use tongs and other utensils not fingers; Do not lick fingers or cooking utensils; Use blue gloves when handling different types of food, e.g. cooked, and raw; Cover any cuts with a protective, waterproof, blue/bright-coloured plaster; Do not wear jewellery; Do not serve food if suffering from illness, sickness, diarrhoea or fever; any other relevant response. **[4]**

2. Cooked meat **[1] Plus two from:** Poultry/cook chill products; Cooked rice; Gravies, stocks, soups and stews; Ice cream; Dairy foods; Named products containing fresh cream; Pâté; Pre-packed sandwiches; Protein-based baby foods; Fish; Raw egg, e.g. in chilled desserts and mayonnaise; Shellfish and seafood / named shellfish or seafood; Soya milk; Unwashed fruit and vegetables. **[2]**

3. **One from:** Digital probe; Food probe; Food thermometer; Meat probe; Meat thermometer; Temperature probe (Do **not** accept just thermometer or probe) **[1]**

4. c) ✓ **[1]**

Food Choices – pages 25–29

Page 25 Food Choices

1. Kosher meat **[1]**
2. Anaphylaxis **underlined** **[1]**
3. Coeliac disease is a condition where people have an adverse reaction to gluten **[1]**, a protein found in wheat, barley, rye, and – to a lesser extent – oats. **[1]** Coeliacs cannot absorb any nutrients if they eat gluten and this can cause severe pain, anaemia and malnutrition. **[1]**
4. Lactose intolerance **[1]**
5. Gluten free – the symbol from Coeliac UK. **[1]**
6.

Religion	Dietary Restriction
Islam **[1]**	No pork
	Only Halal meat
Hinduism **[1]**	No beef or beef products
Christianity **[1]**	No particular dietary restrictions

7. Type 1 usually occurs in childhood and is not associated with excess sugar in the diet or obesity. **[1]** Type 2 generally occurs in adults over 40. **[1]** 90% of people with diabetes have this type. It is linked to obesity and those that have a high sugar diet. **[1]** Both types are controlled with insulin.

Page 26 British and International Cuisines

1. b) ✓ **[1]**
2. Cheddar **[1]**
3.

Country	Dishes	Key Ingredients and Flavours
England	Cornish pasty **[1]**;	A folded pastry with filling (meat, vegetable, cheese) **[1]**;
	Shepherd's pie **[1]**	A layer of meat sauce with mashed potato on top **[1]**
France	Bouillabaisse **[1]**;	Fish soup **[1]**;
	Tarte tatin **[1]**	Sweet apple pie with pastry at bottom **[1]**
Spain	Tortilla **[1]**;	Egg omelette filled with fried potatoes and onion **[1]**;
	Paella **[1]**	Rice with seafood **[1]**
Italy	Minestrone **[1]**;	Soup with small pasta **[1]**;
	Lasagne **[1]**	Layers of pasta and meat/vegetables with white sauce on top **[1]**

4. It is the testing of two similar products. **[1]** There are three samples but two are the same. **[1]** All samples are coded differently. **[1]** The aim is to try and identify the odd one out. **[1]**
5. b) ✓ **[1]**

Page 27 Sensory Evaluation

1. Sensory **analysis [1]** involves using our **five [1]** senses to **evaluate [1]** how much we **like [1]** a dish. We use these senses **together [1]** when we **eat [1]** our food.
2. Taste **[1]** Sight **[1]** Smell/Aroma **[1]** Touch **[1]** Hearing **[1]**
3. Find a quiet area. **[1]** Invite people to taste. **[1]** Provide water to cleanse the palate. **[1]** Code the food samples. **[1]** Use a recording sheet. **[1]** Clean eating implements if required. **[1]**

Page 28 Food Labelling

1. a) ✓ **[1]**
2. Guideline daily amounts **[1]**
3. In descending order with the greatest amount first. **[1]**
4. **Six from:** Name of the product; Weight or volume; Allergen information; Date mark; Storage instructions; Cooking instructions – to ensure the food is safe to eat; Place of origin; Name and address of manufacturer; Batch mark for traceability; Nutritional information on pre-packaged foods **[6]**
5. They must be clearly highlighted in bold or underlined. **[1]** They must be clearly identifiable by the consumer. **[1]**

Page 29 Factors Affecting Food Choice

1. Our enjoyment of food is affected by what the food **looks, [1]** smells **[1]** and **tastes [1]** like.
2. **Any three suitable answers. Examples include:** Christianity – Christmas – Christmas Cake, Christmas Pudding etc; Judaism – Passover – Unleavened bread, Hanukkah, brisket, latkes chicken soup; Islam – Eid – dates eaten to break the fast, al-ache mutton/lamb-based dishes. **[3]**
3. Food is fresher **[1]**; Minimal food miles reducing carbon footprint **[1]**; Supporting local business **[1]**.
4. imported **[1]**
5. **Answer to include discussion relating to:** Special offers; Product placement in the store; In-store promotions; Advertising; Money-off coupons; Recipe cards. **[3]**

Food Provenance – pages 30–34

Page 30 Food and the Environment

1. **Any two suitable answers, for example:** Rissoles **[1]**; Bubble and squeak **[1]**; Soup **[1]**; Corned beef hash **[1]**
2. c) ✓ **[1]**
3. b) ✓ **[1]**
4. Earthworms **[1]** Food waste **[1]**
5. Wise shopping and planning ahead reduces the amount of food bought in the first place **[1]**; FIFO (first-in first-out storage) reduces food wasted **[1]**; Only prepare the food you actually need, so nothing is needlessly thrown away **[1]**; Use food before it goes out

of date, so that food does not have to be thrown away for safety reasons [1]; Use leftover food to make other dishes, thereby avoiding having to throw leftover food out [1]; Do home composting so that any food you have to throw out does not have to be transported to a landfill site [1].

Page 31 Food Provenance and Production Methods

1. c) ✓ [1]
2. Foods produced using nutrient rich liquids instead of soil. [1] Takes place in vast polytunnels or greenhouses [1] with controlled environments [1]. Expensive so only for high end crops. [1]
3. b) ✓ [1] c) ✓ [1]
4. **Five from:** Manufacturer [1]; Producer or grower [1]; Distributer [1]; Transporter [1]; Retailer [1]; Consumer [1]
5. **Any three from:** Fewer small farm communities; A greater number of larger business farms; Large numbers of animals and poultry being kept in massive buildings; and fed on high nutrient feeds in a short period of time, designed to maximise growth; Widespread use of antibiotics, growth enhancers, fertilisers and pesticides; Small farm fields being opened up/ woodland destroyed to make room for large machinery access. [3]

Page 32 Sustainability of Food

1. b) ✓ [1]
2. True [1]
3. a) **Any two from:** The Fairtrade logo means that the farmer in a developing country who produced the goods gets a realistic income [1]; Investment in the local community takes place [1]; There are better working conditions for the producing farmer [1]; A fair price is paid for the goods [1]; Sustainable production methods are used [1].
   b) Possible answers, **any two from:** Chocolate; Tea; Coffee; Bananas **(two answers needed for 1 mark)**.
4. The Red Tractor logo tells us that the food has been produced, processed and packed to the Red Tractor standards [1]; The flag on the Red Tractor logo shows the country of origin [1]; Red Tractor labelling assures good standards of food hygiene and safety [1]; Red Tractor labelling assures high standards of equipment used in production [1]; Red Tractor assures good standards of animal health and welfare [1]; Environmental issues are respected by Red Tractor suppliers [1]; Red Tractor standards ensure responsible use of pesticides [1]. Any product with the Red Tractor logo can be traced from farm to fork [1].

Page 33 Food Production

1. Evaporated milk that has sugar added and is very thick. [1]
2. **Three from:** Single [1]; Whipping [1]; Double [1]; Extra thick [1]
3. a) **Any three suitable answers, e.g. three from:** Red Leicester [1]; Cheddar [1]; Cheshire [1]; Lancashire [1]; Wensleydale [1]; Stilton [1]; Caerphilly [1]
   b) **Any three suitable answers, e.g. three from:** Brie [1]; Camembert [1]; Fromage frais [1]; Roquefort [1]; Saint Agur [1].
4. Durum wheat [1]
5. a) Bran [1]
   b) White flour [1]
6. Lactose intolerant [1] people can substitute animal milk in their diet with milk made from soya, rice, coconut, almond or oats. These milks don't contain lactose. [1] Vegans [1] won't drink milk from an animal. Veganism seeks to avoid causing suffering and pain to animals but it also seeks to avoid their exploitation when it comes to animal-based milks. [1]

Page 34 Food Processing

1. **Four from:** Sunlight [1]; Oven drying [1]; Roller drying [1]; Spray drying [1]; AFD/Accelerated freeze drying [1]
2. a) Milk is heated to 140 degrees for 5 seconds then put into an airtight container. [1] It can then be stored for up to 6 months. [1]
   b) Ultra heat treated [1]
   c) Slight change in taste [1]; Colour remains similar [1]; Little change in nutrients [1]
3. a) Strictly controlled X-rays are passed through the food [1] which delays ripening. [1]
   b) Vitamin A [1], Vitamin C [1], Vitamin E [1], Vitamin K [1] may be lost
   c) Food looks fresh [1] and tastes the same [1]

Pages 35–51 Practice Exam Paper 1

Section A

1.1	B	[1]
1.2	C	[1]
1.3	A	[1]
1.4	C	[1]
2.1	C	[1]
2.2	D	[1]
2.3	C	[1]
2.4	C	[1]
3.1	A	[1]
3.2	B	[1]
3.3	D	[1]
3.4	A	[1]
4.1	C	[1]
4.2	C	[1]
4.3	A	[1]
4.4	B	[1]
5.1	C	[1]
5.2	D	[1]
5.3	A	[1]
5.4	D	[1]

Section B

6.1 To consume the correct nutrients [1]; To consume nutrients in the right proportions [1]; To maintain a healthy weight (correct BMI) [1]; To reduce the risk of diet related disease or named disease (e.g. Type 2 diabetes, heart disease) [1]

6.2 **Three from:** Lack of knowledge of food [1]; Lack of food preparation skills/those with no skills relying on ready meals or takeaways [1]; Financial issues [1]; Lack of time to plan, shop and cook [1]; Family habits, preferences and routines about food [1]; Allergies and intolerances e.g. lactose intolerance [1]

6.3 **Ten from:** Plenty of calcium and vitamin D for her own and baby's bone and tooth development/named good sources of calcium and vitamin D, e.g. dairy products [1]; Look for fortified foods, e.g. breakfast cereals [1]; Consider methods of cooking in order to retain vital nutrients especially water soluble vitamins, e.g. steaming to retain vitamin C [1]; Drinks lots of water to prevent dehydration and help to provide a good milk supply when the baby is born [1]; Take folic acid (often as supplements) during pre- and early pregnancy to reduce risk of spina bifida [1]; Foods not recommended to be eaten in pregnancy include pâté, soft blue cheeses unless cooked, unpasteurised cheeses, with clear explanations linked to harmful bacteria particularly Listeria Monocytogenes [1]; Liver must be avoided because of the high vitamin A content/vitamin A supplements to be avoided [1]; Good supply of fruit and vegetables to provide fibre and vitamin C [1]; Healthy breakfast to avoid snacking [1]; Increase fibre to prevent constipation and haemorrhoids [1]; Iron-rich foods to prevent anaemia and for baby's developing blood supply – 3 months of iron are stored in a newborn baby's liver [1]; Not too many fatty and sugary foods [1]; Only in final three months of pregnancy, extra 200 calories needed per day [1]; Good protein supply for growth of the baby [1]; Important to follow dietary advice given by health professionals, particularly if mother has an underlying health condition [1]; Follow guidance on the Eatwell Guide [1]; Avoid alcohol [1]; Breastfeed to ensure mother–baby bond and to provide newborn baby with immunity benefits of mother's colostrum (first milk) [1]

7.1 **Four from:** Cook to gelatinise the starch (as all raw starch is indigestible) [1]; The hard foods become soft and safe to eat [1]; Cooking softens texture of potatoes [1]; Cooking swells rice and pasta by rehydration/

absorbing water [1]; Starch becomes digestible [1].

7.2 Sauce A has less starch in the roux so will give runnier sauce, therefore better to pour, [1] compared to Sauce B, which has more starch so will be a thicker sauce [1]. Starch gelatinises to thicken when it is heated to boiling. [1]

7.3 Sauce A should have a bigger viscosity circle [1] than Sauce B because it is runnier (less viscous). [1]

7.4

Preparation and cooking stages	Reasons
Peel old potatoes.	*To remove dirt and skin to speed up cooking.*
Chop potatoes.	To reduce size for quicker cooking. [1]
Boil potatoes.	To gelatinise starch and soften potato. [1]
Mash cooked potatoes.	To reduce volume, season and enable mixing with fish. [1]

7.5 Grilling is dry heat, radiated heat [1] that dextrinises potato starch [1], causing golden colour and crisp texture. [1]

8.1 **Six from:** The weight or volume (indicated by 'e', which stands for 'estimated weight' which allows for differences) [1]; Ingredients list from largest to smallest [1]; Allergen information in bold or highlighted [1]; Genetically Modified (GM) ingredients [1]; Date mark – use-by date or best-before date [1]; Storage instructions [1]; Cooking instructions (to ensure the food is safe to eat) [1]; Place of origin [1]; Batch mark for traceability [1]; E numbers – EU approved additives [1]; Nutritional information [1]

8.2 150ml milk; 125ml egg; 100g plain flour; 75g grated cheese; 60g chopped onion; 50g butter; 73ml water **[6 for all in correct order]**

8.3 In case of complaint. [1]

9.1 **Two from:** To make sure the food product meets the consumer's expectations [1]; To find out how a food product compares to similar ones on the market [1]; To check the quality of the product [1]; To ensure the consistency of the product [1]

9.2 The water cleanses the palate between each sample so that the flavours do not influence the results. [1]

9.3 Preference test would be used to see which product would be acceptable to the consumer [1]; The information gathered is very individual as it involves personal preference [1]; A large number of consumers need to be involved [1] to make the test reliable [1]

10.1 Select boiling as a cooking method [1] because pasta needs hydrating [1] to make it swell/become soft/cook [1]

10.2 **Three from:** To ensure even distribution of ingredients [1]; To prevent sticking [1]; To prevent burning/ browning [1]; To prevent lumps/ensure smooth texture [1]; To cook evenly [1]; To achieve the desired/correct consistency [1]; To allow for full gelatinisation/ thickening [1]

10.3 Grilling [1] because radiated heat browns food [1]

10.4 **Four from:** Oven-roasted vegetables are cooked in the oven in fat/oil [1]; Boiling only uses water [1]; Boiling does not brown the vegetables/Oven roasting browns the vegetables [1]; Boiling does not make the vegetables crispy/Oven roasting gives the vegetables a crispy outer [1]; Boiling gives a different flavour to the vegetables than oven roasting gives [1]

11.1 **Two from:** Support British farmers and the economy by buying local (farmers markets, local and regional producers) [1]; Eat more seasonal products (our bodies get the correct nutrients and trace elements that we need at the right time of year) [1]; Buy from suppliers nearer to Britain. [1]

11.2 Transportation around the world has meant that when local seasonal products are not available they can be imported all year round from hotter climates [1]. The transport used creates carbon dioxide gas (CO_2) [1] which is a contributor to global warming [1] and climate change [1]

12.1 There must be ability to track any food, feed, food-producing animal or substance that will be used for consumption. [1] It must be traced back to source [1] to quickly isolate the problem [1] and prevent contaminated products from reaching the customer. [1] All food handlers must have traceability information for suppliers and business [1] Retailers, including caterers, are not required to keep traceability information where they sell to the final consumer. However, where they supply food businesses, all traceability requirements must be adhered to. [1] They must have systems and procedures in place to allow for traceability. [1] Information to be made available to enforcement authorities on demand. [1] They must label or identify food placed on the market to facilitate its traceability. [1] Products of animal origin and sprouted seeds are subject to specific traceability requirements. [1]

Pages 52–68 Practice Exam Paper 2

Section A

1.1	D	[1]
1.2	D	[1]
1.3	B	[1]
1.4	B	[1]
2.1	D	[1]
2.2	D	[1]
2.3	C	[1]
2.4	C	[1]
3.1	B	[1]
3.2	C	[1]
3.3	D	[1]
3.4	C	[1]
4.1	C	[1]
4.2	D	[1]
4.3	D	[1]
4.4	B	[1]
5.1	D	[1]
5.2	C	[1]
5.3	A	[1]
5.4	D	[1]

Section B

6.1 **Two from:** Banana [1]; Blackberries [1]; Blackcurrants [1]; Blueberries [1]; Citrus fruit (or named example of citrus fruit) [1]; Cranberries [1]; Grapes [1]; Guava [1]; Loganberries [1]; Lychee [1]; Mango [1]; Melon [1]; Papaya [1]; Passionfruit [1]; Pineapple [1]; Strawberries [1]; Raspberries [1]

6.2 **Four from:** For the absorption of iron [1]; It is an antioxidant/to support the immune system [1]; To help prevent infection [1]; For healthy gums [1]; To help build strong bones and teeth [1]; To prevent scurvy [1]; To make connective tissue/for the formation of collagen [1]; For healthy skin [1]

6.3 **Four from:** Prepare food quickly just before serving [1]; Use small amounts of boiling water to cook [1]; Only add vegetables to boiling water to cook [1]; Use cooking liquid to make sauces and gravy [1]; Avoid lots of cutting of fruit and vegetables [1]; Tear vegetables rather than cut/use a very sharp knife [1]; Do not overcook vegetables [1]; Use the freshest vegetables possible [1]; Steam rather than boil [1]

6.4 **Six from the following, but must include both advantages and disadvantages:**
Advantages: Can be cheaper/saves money [1]; Can buy slightly imperfect products, saving waste – wonky vegetables [1]; Encourages use of seasonal British foods [1]; Fresher – greater vitamin content [1]; Less time in transit therefore fresher/better quality/better vitamin retention [1]; Easier to buy organic products/ reduced use of pesticides and chemical fertilisers [1]; Environmental considerations [1]; Reduced food miles/carbon footprint/pollution/

energy required to transport food [1]; Often considered to have a better flavour [1]; Supporting local economy/farmers/farm shops/farmers markets [1]; Pick your own farms can provide an educational and fun family activity. [1] **Disadvantages:** Climate – cannot grow certain crops, e.g. bananas, pineapples [1]; Limited variety/seasonally dependent [1]; Limited support for Fairtrade initiatives in developing countries [1]

7.1 Mechanical physical agitation breaks bonds [1] which uncoils the egg white protein [1]; Albumen foams [1] traps air and is denatured. The change is irreversible. [1] **Diagram may show uncoiling of protein, allowing air pockets.**

7.2 Heat causes denaturation of egg proteins [1] and coagulation [1] occurs as proteins clump and solidify [1]; Changes the appearance and texture of the food [1]; Protein sets due to the heat [1]; White coagulates at 60°C/yolk at 70°C [1]

7.3 Lemon juice is acid [1]; It has pH of 2 [1]; Causes clumping of proteins in milk (lactoglobulin, lactalbumen) [1] Curdling occurs [1]; Whey is squeezed out [1]; Denatured protein by acid conditions [1]

8.1 Conduction through the pan base [1]; Convection in the water [1]

8.2 Dry method [1]; Fat-based method [1]; **Any appropriate dishes/recipes cooked each way [2]**

8.3 No added fat [1]; Conserve water soluble nutrients [1]

8.4 [1] (up to maximum of [3]) per correct use of data in each different cooking method. [1] (up to a maximum of [3])

per accurate comparison, e.g. amount of fat added by the method; Vitamin C loss into water; Water soluble vitamin C retained by fat-based method.

9.1 High-risk foods are easily contaminated by bacteria [1] and so can cause food poisoning if not correctly stored at a temperature of 0°C–5°C [1] and cooked thoroughly [1]; They have a short shelf life [1]; High-risk foods include foods which are not cooked before being eaten so, if contaminated, the bacteria will not be destroyed, for example, cream, cooked meats, raw fish (for sushi), quiche [1]; Protein foods such as meat, poultry, eggs, milk and fish are high-risk foods as is cooked rice and pasta. Other high-risk foods are moist foods such as gravy, soup and unpasteurised food, for example soft cheese [1]

9.2 Ensure the probe is clean by using an antibacterial wipe before and after use [1]; Before use, make sure the probe has been calibrated and reset to 0°C [1]; Check the centre or thickest part of the chicken with the probe [1]; Check that the temperature has reached 72°C for at least 2 minutes to ensure bacteria have been killed. [1]

10.1 **Two from:** Ultra-Heat Treated (UHT) [1]; Sterilised [1]; Canned [1]

10.2 Skimmed milk is pasteurised but has had all or most of the fat removed [1]; Semi-skimmed milk is pasteurised but has had some of the fat removed. [1]

10.3 **Four from:** Soya [1]; Rice [1]; Coconut [1]; Almond [1]; Oat [1]

10.4 **Four from:** They are dairy free/100% plant based, and plant-based foods are better for the planet because

they use fewer natural resources [1]; Reducing consumption of saturated fat contributes to the maintenance of normal blood cholesterol levels [1]; Usually fortified with calcium to aid strong healthy bones [1]; They are all lactose free so suitable for those people who are intolerant to lactose (a form of sugar found in milk) [1]; They are also suitable for vegans who do not consume animal products [1]; They are usually fortified and nutrient enhanced [1]

11.1 Allows poultry or animals access to outdoor areas for part of their lives. [1]

11.2 **Three from:** More ethical [1]; Lower negative environmental impact [1]; Animals have better quality meat [1]; Egg laying hens produce more nutritious and tasty eggs [1]

11.3 **Two suitable answers, e.g.** chicken, eggs, pork, beef. [2]

11.4 **Three from:** An environment similar to intensively farmed chicken [1]; Access to natural light from windows [1]; Lower density of birds per square metre than intensively farmed chickens [1]; They have some environmental enrichment such as fresh straw. [1]

11.5 Produce is grown naturally without chemical or synthetic treatments [1]; Natural composts and manure used as fertilisers [1]; They are GM free [1]

Notes

Notes

Acknowledgements

The author and publisher are grateful to the copyright holders for permission to use quoted materials and images.

p.4 Bridge hold and claw grip. This resource was developed for the DfE Licence to Cook programme 2007-2011. © Crown copyright 2007. http://www.nationalarchives.gov.uk/doc/open-government-licence/version/3/

All other images © Shutterstock.com

Every effort has been made to trace copyright holders and obtain their permission for the use of copyright material. The author and publisher will gladly receive information enabling them to rectify any error or omission in subsequent editions. All facts are correct at time of going to press.

Published by Collins
An imprint of HarperCollinsPublishers Ltd
1 London Bridge Street
London SE1 9GF

HarperCollinsPublishers
1st Floor, Watermarque Building, Ringsend Road, Dublin 4, Ireland

© HarperCollinsPublishers Limited 2022

This edition published 2022

ISBN 9780008535087

10 9 8 7 6 5 4 3 2 1

All rights reserved. No part of this publication may be reproduced, stored in a retrieval system, or transmitted, in any form or by any means, electronic, mechanical, photocopying, recording or otherwise, without the prior permission of Collins.

British Library Cataloguing in Publication Data.

A CIP record of this book is available from the British Library.

Authored by: Fiona Balding, Barbara Monks, Barbara Rathmill and Suzanne Gray with Louise T. Davies
Commissioning Editor: Clare Souza
Project Editor: Katie Galloway
Cover Design: Kevin Robbins and Sarah Duxbury
Inside Concept Design: Sarah Duxbury and Paul Oates
Text Design and Layout: Jouve India Private Limited
Production: Lyndsey Rogers
Printed and bound in the UK using 100% Renewable Electricity at CPI Group (UK) Ltd

Published in association with the Food Teachers Centre.

MIX
Paper from
responsible source
FSC™ C007454

This book is produced from independently certified FSC™ paper to ensure responsible forest management.

For more information visit: www.harpercollins.co.uk/green